3

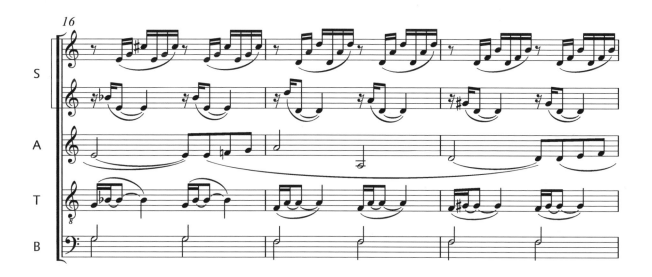

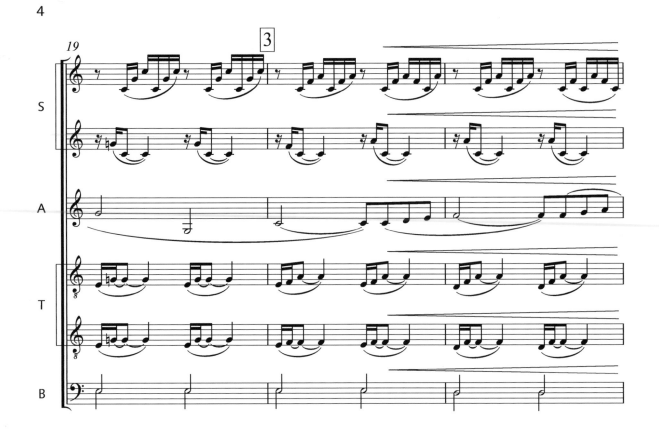

(bocca chiusa)

M -

A -

Johann Sebastian Bach / Charles Gounod /
Rodion Shchedrin

Ave Maria

Transcription for Mixed Choir (SSATTBB) a cappella
Transkription für gemischten Chor (SSATTBB) a cappella

Score / Partitur

SKR 20059

Ave Maria

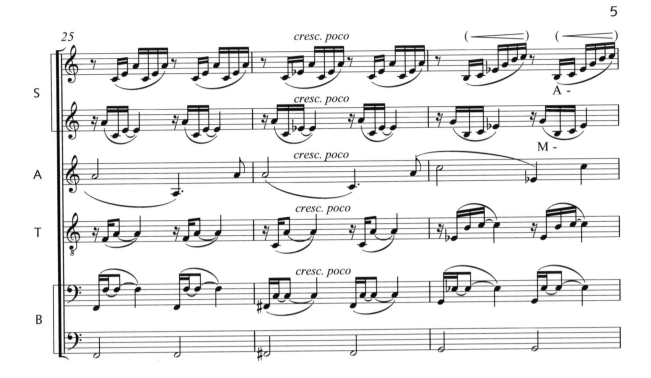

(A-)

(A - *come sopra*)

Schott Music, Mainz 53 486

DISTRIBUTED IN NORTH AND SOUTH AMERICA
EXCLUSIVELY BY

HAL LEONARD
C O R P O R A T I O N

49018172

ISMN 979-0-001-16885-4   SKR 20059